I0448801

September 2013

FEDERAL DATA TRANSPARENCY

Opportunities Remain to Incorporate Lessons Learned as Availability of Spending Data Increases

GAO-13-758

September 2013

FEDERAL DATA TRANSPARENCY

Opportunities Remain to Incorporate Lessons Learned as Availability of Spending Data Increases

Highlights of GAO-13-758, a report to congressional requesters

Why GAO Did This Study

The federal government spends more than $3.7 trillion annually, with more than $1 trillion awarded through contracts, grants, and loans. Improving transparency of spending is essential to improve accountability. Recent federal laws have required increased public information on federal awards and spending. GAO was asked to review current efforts to improve transparency. This report examines (1) transparency efforts under way and (2) the extent to which new initiatives address lessons learned from the Recovery Act. GAO reviewed relevant legislation, executive orders, OMB circulars and guidance, and previous GAO work, including work on Recovery Act reporting. GAO also interviewed officials from OMB, the GAT Board, and other federal entities; government reform advocates; associations representing fund recipients; and a variety of contract and grant recipients.

What GAO Recommends

GAO recommends that the Director of OMB, with the GAT Board, develop a long-term plan to implement comprehensive transparency reform, and increase efforts for obtaining stakeholder input to ensure reporting challenges are addressed. Further, Congress should consider legislating transparency requirements and establishing clear authority to implement these requirements to ensure that recommended approaches for improving transparency are carried out across the federal government. The GAT Board, OMB and other cognizant agencies generally concurred with GAO's recommendations and provided further information, which was incorporated into the report as appropriate.

View GAO-13-758. For more information, contact Stanley J. Czerwinski, (202) 512-6806, czerwinskis@gao.gov

What GAO Found

Several federal entities, including the Government Accountability and Transparency Board (GAT Board), the Recovery Accountability and Transparency Board (Recovery Board), and the Office of Management and Budget (OMB), have initiatives under way to improve the accuracy and availability of federal spending data. The GAT Board, through its working groups, developed approaches to standardize key data elements to improve data integrity; link financial management systems with award systems to reconcile spending data with obligations; and leverage existing data to help improve oversight. With no dedicated funding, GAT Board plans are incremental and leverage ongoing agency initiatives designed to improve existing business processes as well as improve data transparency. These initiatives are in an early stage, and some progress has been made to bring greater consistency to award identifiers. The GAT Board's mandate is to provide strategic direction, not to implement changes. Further, while these early plans are being developed with input from a range of federal stakeholders, the GAT Board and OMB have not developed mechanisms for obtaining input from non-federal fund recipients.

Lessons from implementing the transparency objectives of the Recovery Act could help inform these new initiatives:

- **Standardize data to integrate systems and enhance accountability.** Similar to the GAT Board's current focus on standardization, the Recovery Board recognized that standardized data would be more usable by the public and the Recovery Board for identifying potential misuse of federal funds. However, reporting requirements under the Recovery Act had to be met quickly. Because agencies did not collect spending data in a consistent manner, the most expedient approach was to collect data from fund recipients, even though similar data already existed in agency systems. Given the longer timeframes to develop current transparency initiatives, OMB and the GAT Board are working toward greater data consistency by focusing on data standards. Their plans, however, do not include long-term steps, such as working toward uniform award identifiers that would improve award tracking with less burden on recipients.
- **Obtain stakeholder involvement as reporting requirements are developed.** During the Recovery Act, federal officials listened to the concerns of recipients and made changes to guidance in response, which helped ensure they could meet those requirements. Without similar outreach under current initiatives, reporting challenges may not be addressed, potentially impairing the data's accuracy and completeness, and increasing burden on those reporting.
- **Delineate clear requirements and lines of authority for implementing transparency initiatives.** Unlike the present efforts to expand spending transparency, the Recovery Act provided OMB and the Recovery Board with clear authority and mandated reporting requirements. Given this clarity, transparency provisions were carried out successfully and on time. Going forward, without clear, legislated authority and requirements, the ability to sustain progress and institutionalize transparency initiatives may be jeopardized as priorities shift over time.

_____ **United States Government Accountability Office**

Contents

Abbreviations

CAOC	Chief Acquisition Officers Council
CIGIE	Council of the Inspectors General on Integrity and Efficiency
COFAR	Council on Financial Assistance Reform
DATA	Digital Accountability and Transparency Act
DOD	Department of Defense
FAR	Federal Acquisition Regulation
FFATA	Federal Funding Accountability and Transparency Act of 2006
FPDS-NG	Federal Procurement Data System-Next Generation
GAT Board	Government Accountability and Transparency Board
GRIP	Grants Reporting Information Project
GSA	General Services Administration
HHS	Health and Human Services
OFFM	Office of Federal Financial Management
OFPP	Office of Federal Procurement Policy
OMB	Office of Management and Budget
Recovery Act	American Recovery and Reinvestment Act of 2009
Recovery Board	Recovery Accountability and Transparency Board
ROC	Recovery Operations Center

U.S. GOVERNMENT ACCOUNTABILITY OFFICE

441 G St. N.W.
Washington, DC 20548

September 12, 2013

Congressional Requesters:

The federal government spends more than $3.7 trillion annually. Of that, more than $1 trillion is awarded through contracts, grants, and loans, and an additional $1 trillion is forgone in tax revenues through tax expenditures.[1] Transparency—shedding light on the amount of spending, what it is spent on, who receives the funds, and what are the results of that spending—is essential to improving government accountability and fostering civic engagement. Within the last decade, Congress and the administration have taken several steps to improve the transparency of federal spending data, including the passage of two statutes intended to expand public access to information on federal programs. The first, the Federal Funding Accountability and Transparency Act of 2006 (FFATA), required the establishment of an information website on grant and contract awards and subawards.[2] Today, this federal agency and subrecipient information is available at www.USAspending.gov. The second, the American Recovery and Reinvestment Act of 2009 (Recovery Act), required that recipients' reports on award and spending data be made available on a website.[3] Today, this information is accessible at www.Recovery.gov. These transparency efforts have enabled civic engagement, and have allowed the public—from ordinary citizens to sophisticated data users—to access information on spending, recipients, and uses of funds. The data's availability has also provided opportunities for increased oversight to prevent and detect fraud, waste, and abuse of federal funds, and to improve the efficiency and effectiveness of federal spending.

While many believe that the transparency of federal spending data has increased, both the administration and members of Congress have

---

[1]For the purpose of this report federal spending data includes all federal expenditures or obligations for grants, salaries and wages, procurement contracts, direct payments for individuals, and other direct payments, plus commitments in the form of direct loans, guaranteed or insured loans, and insurance.

[2]Pub. L. No. 109-282, 120 Stat. 1186 (2006), as amended by Pub. L. No. 110-252, § 6202(a), 122 Stat. 2323, 2387 (2008) (*codified at* 31 U.S.C. § 6101 note).

[3]Pub. L. No. 111-5, §§ 1512, 1526, 123 Stat. 115, 287–288, 293–294 (2009).

suggested the need for more transparency. At present, USAspending.gov only provides data on funds awarded; the site does not include information on disbursements. In terms of data collection, federal agencies and recipients report to various systems, sometimes with the same information and, as a result, direct unnecessary time and resources to administrative activities. In addition, the lack of consistent data structures prevents easy aggregation of data at the government-wide level, hampering the ability to link existing financial, award, and procurements systems. It also increases the cost of government transactions and the burden on federal fund recipients. And, as we have reported previously, the accuracy and reliability of the data needs to be improved.[4] Emerging transparency efforts include specific changes in data collection under consideration by the Government Accountability and Transparency Board (GAT Board), newly-created under a June 2011 Executive Order.[5] Further, proposed legislation has been introduced in the House and the Senate designed to improve the transparency of federal spending data.[6]

Given these various initiatives under way, you asked us to examine federal efforts to increase the transparency of federal spending data, and identify lessons from the experience of operating existing data systems that could contribute to these efforts. We examined (1) federal initiatives to improve the accuracy and availability of federal spending data and (2) the extent to which lessons identified by us and federal fund recipients from the operation of Recovery.gov and USAspending.gov are being addressed by these new transparency initiatives.

To address these objectives we examined data collection and reporting requirements under FFATA and the Recovery Act; the June 2011 Executive Order related to transparency; relevant Office of Management and Budget (OMB) guidance; and action plans created by the GAT Board, Recovery Board, and other federal entities with responsibility for

---

[4]See, for example, GAO, *Electronic Government: Implementation of the Federal Funding Accountability and Transparency Act of 2006*, GAO-10-365 (Washington, D.C.: Mar. 12, 2010).

[5]Executive Order 13,576, "Delivering an Efficient, Effective, and Accountable Government," 76 Fed. Reg. 35,297 (June 16, 2011).

[6]Digital Accountability and Transparency Act of 2013, H.R. 2061, 113th Cong. (2013); Digital Accountability and Transparency Act of 2013, S. 994, 113th Cong. (2013).

developing approaches to improve federal data transparency. We interviewed officials at OMB, the GAT Board, and the Recovery Board who are examining new data transparency initiatives. We also interviewed officials at three agencies who are developing new transparency prototypes within their agencies: the Department of Defense (DOD), the Department of Health and Human Services (HHS), and the Department of Treasury (Treasury), respectively. We also interviewed officials at the General Services Administration (GSA), the agency that manages USAspending.gov. To get their perspectives on lessons learned from both the operation of existing transparency systems and federal efforts under way to improve data transparency, we spoke with officials from organizations representing federal fund recipients and government reform organizations.[7] We also conducted seven focus groups with federal fund recipients representing state and local governments, nonprofit organizations, higher education research institutions, and private businesses who receive grants from, or contracted with, the federal government. Finally, we reviewed our previous work on the reporting successes and challenges experienced by both agencies and federal fund recipients. This step allowed us to identify lessons learned from those experiences that should be considered as new approaches to data transparency are developed. Although we spoke with numerous affected entities and stakeholders with opinions on transparency, our work should not be considered to be generalizeable to all who have opinions about these issues.

We conducted this performance audit from November 2012 to September 2013 in accordance with generally accepted government auditing standards. Those standards require that we plan and perform the audit to obtain sufficient, appropriate evidence to provide a reasonable basis for our findings and conclusions based on our audit objectives. We believe that the evidence obtained provides a reasonable basis for our findings

---

[7]For this review, we interviewed and collected comments from officials at the following organizations: National Association of State Auditors, Comptrollers, and Treasurers; National Association of State Budget Officers; National Association of Counties; Federal Demonstration Partnership; National Council of Nonprofits; National Association of State Chief Information Officers; Council on Government Relations; Professional Services Council; Center for Effective Government; Project on Government Oversight; and Sunlight Foundation. We selected these associations because our preliminary research indicated that they had either been involved in Recovery Act implementation, had published reports related to the Recovery Act, or had expressed official positions on existing transparency systems.

and conclusions based on our audit objectives. For more information on our objectives, scope, and methodology, see appendix I.

Background

Between 2006 and 2011, Congress initiated two significant efforts to increase public awareness of, and access to, federal spending data: the Federal Funding Accountability and Transparency Act of 2006 (FFATA), and the American Recovery and Reinvestment Act of 2009 (Recovery Act). Both acts mandated the creation of public-access websites, which involved a broad range of data-collection and data-reporting activities, and required OMB and federal agencies, among others, to address multiple levels of accountability and transparency. The passage of FFATA was part of a series of legislative and executive branch efforts to make comprehensive data on federal awards available to the public. Congress passed FFATA in 2006 to increase the transparency of and accountability for the more than $1 trillion in contracts and financial assistance awarded annually by federal agencies. Among other things, the act required OMB to establish a free, publicly accessible web site containing data on federal awards (e.g., contracts, loans, and grants) no later than January 1, 2008. In addition, the act required OMB to include data on subawards by January 1, 2009 and authorized OMB to provide guidance and instruction to agencies to ensure the existence and operation of the website, and required agencies to comply with that guidance. OMB launched the web site—www.USASpending.gov—in December 2007. However, in 2010, we reported that the award data in USAspending.gov was not always complete or reliable.[8]

To improve the quality of the data reported on USAspending.gov, OMB issued guidance under the Open Government Directive that directed agencies to (1) designate a high-level senior official to be accountable for the quality of federal spending information disseminated on public websites; (2) establish a data quality framework for federal spending information, including a governance structure, risk assessments, control activities, and monitoring program; and (3) submit plans to OMB for addressing these requirements.[9] OMB also issued guidance to agencies on improving the data quality of the Federal Procurement Data System-Next Generation (FPDS-NG), and established a deadline for the agencies

---

[8]GAO-10-365.

[9]OMB, *Open Government Directive*, M-10-06 (Washington, D.C.: Dec. 8, 2009).

to collect subaward data.[10] FPDS-NG is a contract database that is one of the main sources of USAspending.gov data.

In crafting the Recovery Act, Congress and the administration envisioned an unprecedented level of transparency into federal spending data. The act required recipients of Recovery Act funds to submit quarterly reports with information on each project or activity, including the amount and use of funds and an estimate of the number of jobs created and the number of jobs retained. Similar to FFATA, the Recovery Act called for the establishment of a website that would give the public access to information on the many projects and activities funded under the act. The Recovery Accountability and Transparency Board launched the Recovery.gov site in 2009 to fulfill these requirements. In addition, a second site—www.FederalReporting.gov—was established for recipients to report their data. Recipients first reported in early October 2009 on the period from February through September 2009. Reporting has continued for each quarter since then.

More recently, in June 2011, the administration issued Executive Order 13576 "Delivering an Efficient, Effective, and Accountable Government." The order, among other things, established the GAT Board to provide strategic direction for enhancing transparency of federal spending data. The GAT Board was also charged with advancing efforts to detect fraud, waste, and abuse of federal programs. Its 11 members include agency inspectors general, agency chief financial officers, a senior OMB official and other such members as the President shall designate. The GAT Board is mandated to work with the Recovery Board to build on lessons learned from the Recovery Act's implementation.

---

[10]OMB, *Improving Acquisition Data Quality for Fiscal Years 2009 and 2010* (Washington, D.C.: Oct. 7, 2009).

Figure 1: Timeline of Selected Data Transparency Initiatives

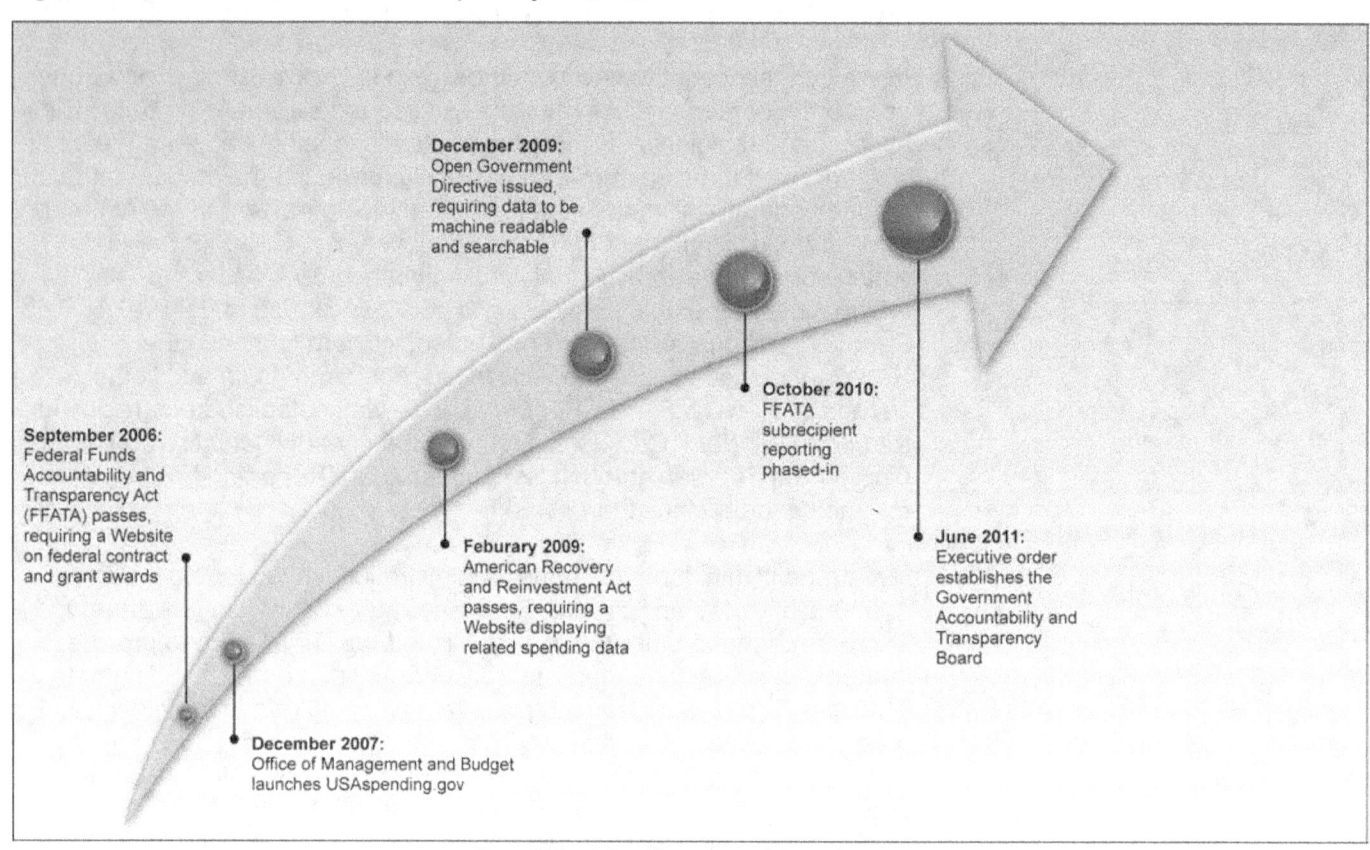

September 2006:
Federal Funds
Accountability and
Transparency Act
(FFATA) passes,
requiring a Website
on federal contract
and grant awards

December 2007:
Office of Management and Budget
launches USAspending.gov

Feburary 2009:
American Recovery
and Reinvestment Act
passes, requiring a
Website displaying
related spending data

December 2009:
Open Government
Directive issued,
requiring data to be
machine readable
and searchable

October 2010:
FFATA
subrecipient
reporting
phased-in

June 2011:
Executive order
establishes the
Government
Accountability and
Transparency
Board

Source: GAO analysis and Recovery.gov website.

USAspending.gov and Recovery.gov rely on different sources of information, and make different types of data available to the public. USAspending.gov provides information on federal award obligations, including the recipient's name, funding agency, amount of award, and descriptive title. It relies primarily on data submitted by federal agencies and, to some extent, by recipients. In addition, agencies use different reporting platforms to submit information about contract and grant awards. In contrast, Recovery.gov, which relies primarily on information submitted by recipients, provides information on federal award expenditures, including information on each project or activity funded, the amount and use of funds, and an estimate of the jobs funded.

GAO-13-758 Federal Spending Data Transparency

The USAspending.gov website draws data from different data sources, as shown in figure 2.

- The Federal Procurement Data System-Next Generation: Procurement data are imported from this system, which collects information on contract actions, procurement trends, and achievement of socioeconomic goals, such as small business participation. OMB was responsible for establishing the system, and GSA administers it. Since 1980, FPDS-NG and its predecessor FPDS have been the primary government-wide databases for contracting information. Federal agencies are responsible for ensuring the information reported in this database is complete and accurate.
- The Data Submission and Validation Tool: Data on financial assistance awards (grants, loans, loan guarantees, cooperative agreements and other assistance) are provided by federal agencies and are transmitted directly to GSA via this tool. As with FPDS-NG, federal agencies are responsible for ensuring the information reported in this database is complete and accurate.
- The FFATA Subaward Reporting System: Contractors and grant recipients use this tool to capture and report subaward and executive compensation data regarding their first-tier subawards to meet the FFATA reporting requirements. Contractors and grant recipients are required to file a report within a specified timeframe after making a subaward greater than $25,000 and they are responsible for ensuring information reported to this database is complete and accurate.

Figure 2: USAspending.gov Data Sources

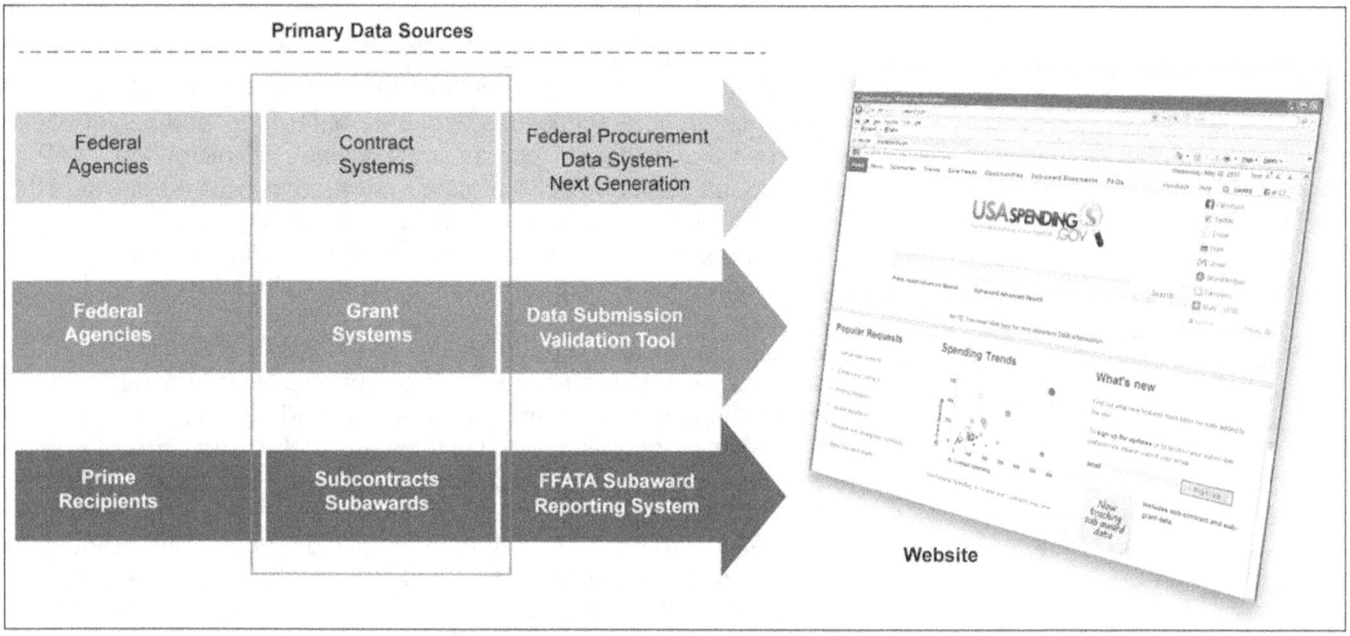

Source: GAO analysis and USAspending.gov website.

In contrast to USAspending.gov, Recovery.gov's data are collected from federal fund recipients. Section 1512 of the Recovery Act requires recovery fund recipients to report quarterly on Recovery Act-related spending. Recipients provide their information to the agency through FederalReporting.gov. Agencies, then, review the data provided. The validated data are then published on Recovery.gov, as illustrated by figure 3.

GAO-13-758 Federal Spending Data Transparency

Figure 3: Recovery.gov Data Sources

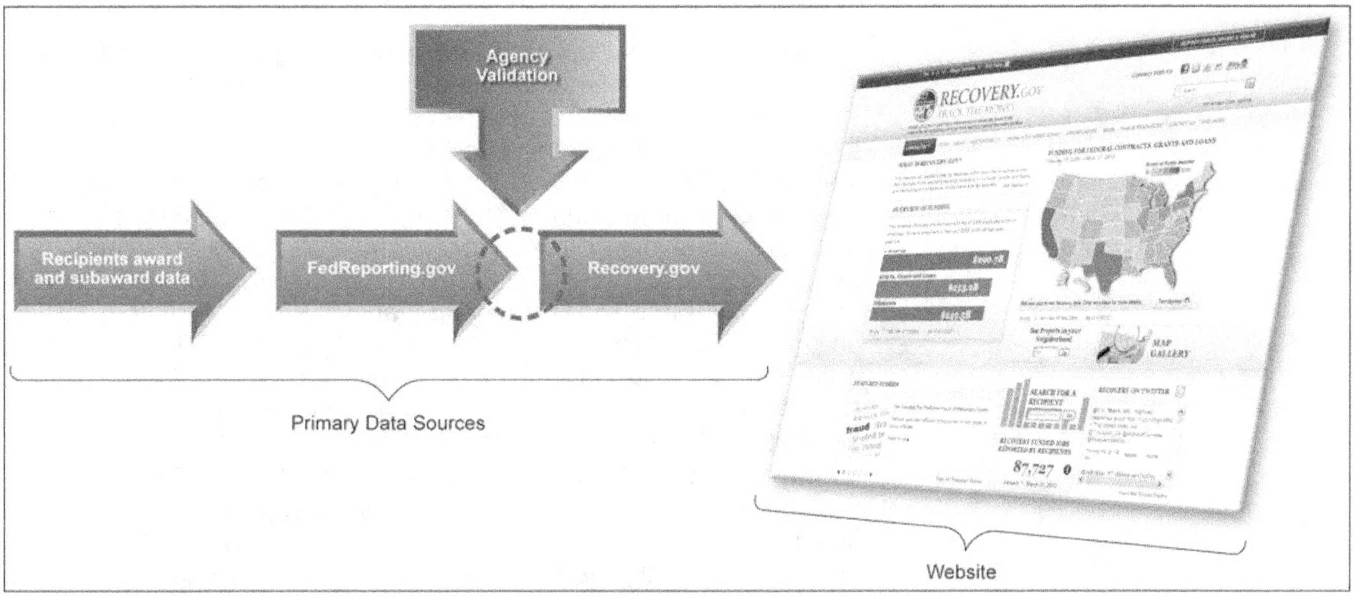

Source: GAO analysis and Recovery.gov website.

Transparency Efforts Under Way Focus On Standardizing Data to Integrate Systems and Enhance Spending Oversight

With Its Role Limited to Providing Strategic Direction, the GAT Board Is Leveraging Ongoing Agency Initiatives for Implementation

The GAT Board's role is to provide strategic direction for enhancing federal spending transparency. Along with OMB and the Recovery Board, it oversees several ongoing government-wide initiatives designed to expand the transparency of federal spending data. As part of its role to provide strategic direction, the GAT Board established four work groups in 2012 and 2013 (see figure 4). These groups are charged with developing approaches for improving transparency across three functional areas—procurement, grants, and financial management—and expanding data availability to improve spending oversight. Work group members represent the federal procurement, grants, financial management, and oversight communities. The members are set up to leverage the collective expertise of several interagency forums.

- **Procurement Data Standardization and Integrity Working Group:** The work group was established to identify approaches for standardizing contract data elements and electronic transactions to ensure data are accurate and contract transactions can be tracked from purchase order through vendor payment. As the federal government's largest contracting agency, DOD is a lead agency on this work group, along with members of OMB's Office of Federal Procurement Policy (OFPP). The Procurement Work Group initiative grew out of OMB's and DOD's long-standing efforts to improve the accuracy of contract data that agencies submit to FPDS-NG. Work group members also include representatives from the Chief Acquisition Officers Council, an interagency forum of agency acquisition officers.[11]

- **Grants Data Standardization and Integrity Working Group:** The work group has been tasked with developing approaches to standardize grants data elements to achieve greater consistency across the federal government. HHS, along with OMB's Office of Federal Financial Management (OFFM), provides leadership to this work group. Members also include representatives from the newly established Council on Financial Assistance Reform (COFAR).[12] According to HHS officials, the group's efforts build on the agency's prior work with the Grants Policy Council and the Grants Executive Board to standardize and streamline grant procedures.[13]

- **Financial Management Integration and Data Integrity Working Group:** The GAT Board, in conjunction with Treasury, is examining approaches for linking the financial management data maintained in agency financial systems with agency awards data in order to improve the quality of data displayed to the public. The GAT Board established this work group to align with Treasury's ongoing efforts to define their data vision and approach, including a proposal to move the

---

[11]The council consists of executive branch acquisition professionals and was established to provide a senior level forum for monitoring and improving the federal acquisition system. 41 U.S.C. §§ 1311–1312.

[12]OMB, *Creation of the Council on Financial Assistance Reform*, M-12-01 (Washington, D.C.: Oct. 27, 2011).

[13]The Grants Policy Council and the Grants Executive Board were replaced by COFAR in 2011.

administrative responsibility for USAspending.gov from the GSA to Treasury. While the GAT Board is responsible for setting direction and developing strategy, the Board is leveraging Treasury's on-going modernization efforts with assistance from OFFM.

- **Data Analytics Working Group:** The work group was formed in response to the executive order establishing the GAT Board, which required the board to advance efforts to detect and remediate fraud, waste, and abuse in federal programs. The group is under the direction of the Inspector General of the United States Postal Service and has representatives from the Recovery Board. The group also provides information about its activities with the Council of Inspectors General for Integrity and Efficiency.[14] The working group's goal is to expand on the Recovery Board's Recovery Operation Center (ROC) for improving fraud detection in federal spending.

The GAT Board, through its working groups, is in the process of determining approaches for carrying out its mission. However, its mandate is only to develop strategy, not to implement it. The GAT Board relies on the working groups' lead agencies to develop recommendations and implement approaches that it has approved. Moreover, with no dedicated funding, the GAT Board's strategic plan is short-term and calls for an incremental approach that builds upon ongoing agency initiatives. These initiatives include efforts to modernize systems or improve agency management, designed to improve existing business processes as well as improve data transparency.[15] The GAT Board's initial plans largely focus on efforts at the federal level and some progress has been made to bring greater consistency to award identifiers.[16]

---

[14]The Council of Inspectors General on Integrity and Efficiency is an independent entity within the executive branch. It was established to address integrity, economy, and effectiveness issues that transcend individual government agencies. The council also is charged with increasing the professionalism and effectiveness of personnel by developing policies, standards, and approaches to aid in establishing a well-trained and highly-skilled workforce in the offices of the Inspectors General. Inspector General Reform Act of 2008, Pub. L. No. 110-409, § 7, 122 Stat. 4302, 4305–4313 (2008) (*codified at* 5 U.S.C. App. 3, § 11 (Inspector General Act of 1978)).

[15] The GAT Board's strategic plan establishes a set of goals for calendar year 2013. See: The Government and Transparency Board, *Way Forward for Calendar Year 2013* (Washington, D.C: Mar. 27, 2013).

[16]An award identifier is typically alphanumeric and used by agencies to collect financial information, keep track of progress of awards and whether recipients are meeting award program requirements, and for invoices, payment requests, and payments.

Figure 4: Government Accountability Transparency Board and Work Group Agency Partners.

Directions:

Roll over each GAT Board seat at the table and each Work Group listed in the chart below to see more information regarding the member agencies.

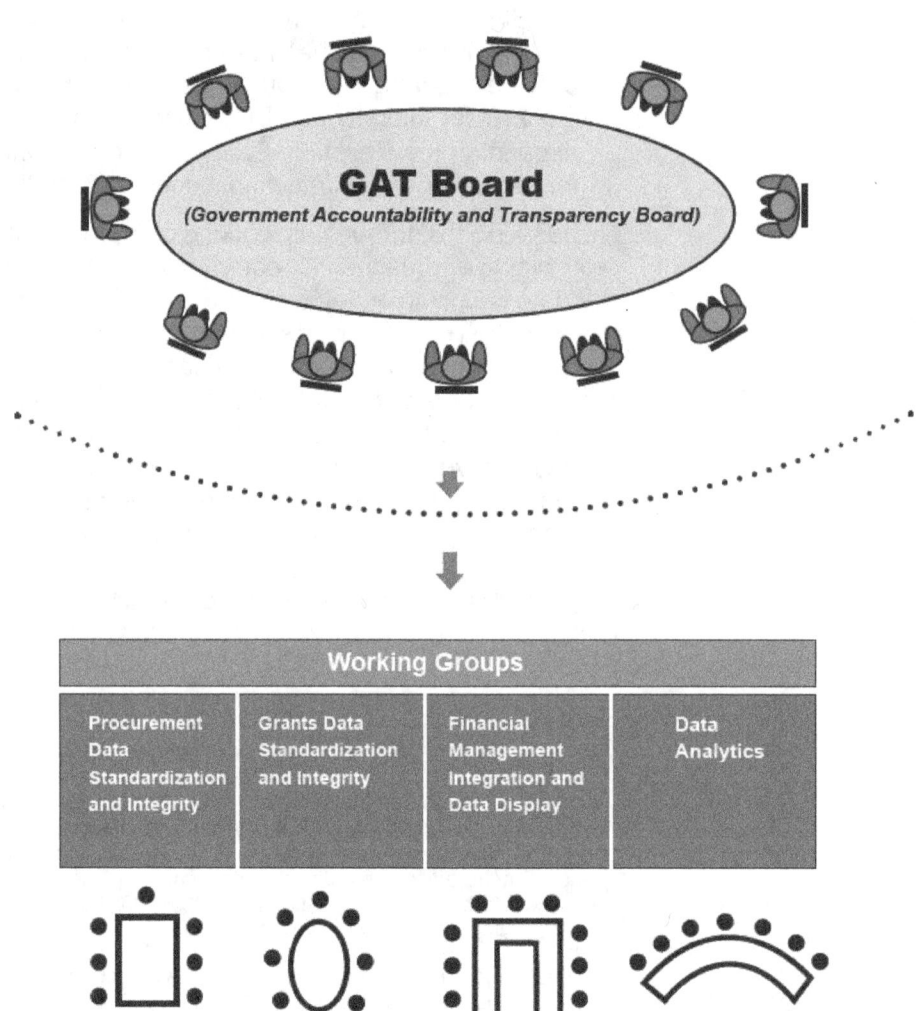

Print instructions | To print text version of this graphic, go to appendix II.

Page 12

GAO-13-758 Federal Spending Data Transparency

Efforts Are Under Way to Standardize Key Data Elements So That Data Integrity is Improved

Data standardization and a uniform convention for identifying contract and grant awards throughout their life cycle are the first steps in ensuring data quality and tracking spending data. The GAT Board's December 2011 Report to the President notes that introducing greater consistency into the award process will help better reconcile spending information from multiple sources and allow for more effective analysis and oversight.[17] Currently, efforts under way are aimed at introducing more consistency into the way federal spending data are reported, collected, and publically displayed. Initial efforts are focused on identifying approaches to standardize contract and grant data elements. These efforts are intended to improve the accuracy of spending data, link award data to payment data to help track awards throughout the life cycle, and advance efforts to detect and remediate fraud, waste, and abuse. While these efforts are largely in the early stages of development, progress has been made to establish more uniform award identifiers, and to test the plausibility of using data standards and a centralized data-collection portal to minimize the burden of federal fund recipients.

According to GAT Board officials, efforts to standardize and improve the integrity of contract data are being advanced through a series of Federal Acquisition Regulatory (FAR) Council rulemakings.[18] In particular, DOD developed a proposal based in part on work of the GAT Board for the FAR Council to consider a uniform procurement identifier—a number that could be attached to a contract so it can be tracked throughout the procurement process. The recently proposed FAR regulation will require federal agencies to use unique procurement instrument identifiers starting no later than October 1, 2014, for all new solicitations and awards. To further standardize procurement transactions across the federal government, the proposed rule also calls for the implementation of a uniform procurement instrument identifier system as the unique identifier

---

[17]The Government Accountability and Transparency Board, *Report and Recommendations to the President* (Washington, D.C.: December 2011).

[18]The members of the FAR Council jointly issue and maintain a single government-wide procurement regulation, known as FAR. The FAR Council's membership consists of the OFPP Administrator for Federal Procurement Policy, the Secretary of Defense, the Administrator of the National Aeronautics and Space Administration, and the GSA Administrator. The Council manages, coordinates, controls, and monitors the maintenance of, issuance of, and changes in, FAR. 41 U.S.C. §§ 1301–1304. The FAR Council periodically publishes rules implementing changes to the FAR. A final rule is typically preceded by a proposed rule, published in the *Federal Register* and seeking public comments.

for all contracting offices.[19] This would enable a contract to be tracked across various systems and across its life cycle.

OMB, in consultation with the GAT Board, has issued new guidance that requires all federal agencies to establish unique identification numbers for financial assistance awards. It also mandates agencies to check the accuracy of spending information against an official record of agency accounts.[20] While this guidance could help bring greater consistency to grant award data, it only requires agencies to assign award numbers unique within their agency to grant transactions. Thus, the guidance does not provide the same level of uniformity as is required for contracts nor does it provide uniformity across all contract and financial assistance spending. Agencies and even subunits of agencies use inconsistent award-numbering systems. These respective systems are created to conform to their own internal agency management systems to identify contracts, grants, and loans. In many agencies, there is no direct link or continuous use of one standard award identifier between systems and offices. The disparate award identification systems and naming conventions used by agencies today make the task of reporting and tracking spending data inefficient and burdensome. Recovery Board officials raised some concerns, noting that a lack of uniform standards for identifying grants would make it difficult to pre-populate recipient reports with information from the awarding agency, and reconcile obligation with award data. While this lack of uniformity may not optimize the use of the data, OMB has noted that, in combination with other information provided, it will uniquely identify a given grant. Further, in their oral comments on our draft report, an OMB staff member told us that standardizing an identifier format could cause problems for agency systems because some agencies structure their award identifiers to track particular characteristics of grants for their internal use. Therefore, OMB has issued this guidance and then will evaluate the improvements in light of the added resources needed to implement them.

---

[19]78 Fed. Reg. 34,020 (June 6, 2013).

[20]The June 12, 2013, memorandum, "Improving Data Quality for USAspending.gov," requires all federal agencies to (1) assign financial assistance award identification numbers unique within the Federal agency; and (2) identify and implement a process to compare and validate USAspending.gov funding information with data in the agency's financial system.

GAO-13-758 Federal Spending Data Transparency

As part of its work with the Grants Data Standardization and Integrity Working Group, HHS recently completed a preliminary analysis to determine the degree to which grants data elements are standardized across the federal government. According to the chair of the GAT Board, it is currently more challenging to standardize grants data elements because, unlike FAR's uniform procurement regulations, there is no single set of grant regulations in use across the federal government.

The Recovery Accountability and Transparency Board recently concluded a proof-of-concept project that tests the feasibility of using FederalReporting.gov, to collect data on non-Recovery Act grant expenditures. In a pilot involving nine grant recipients and two federal agencies,[21] the Grant Reporting Information Project (GRIP) captured data elements from OMB's standardized grant expenditure reporting form Standard Form 425, as well as subrecipient and vendor expense data. GRIP also tested whether such a system could lessen reporting burden and improve the accuracy of the data submitted by fund recipients. In addition, the pilot tested whether the use of a universal award identification number could be used to track grant expenditures throughout the grant life cycle. The Recovery Board's analysis of the GRIP project found that feedback from the pilot participants supported using FederalReporting.gov for grant reporting. The analysis also validated the effectiveness of using a universal award identifier.[22] In addition, the board's analysis found that, while such features as machine-readable formats and pre-populated data fields helped the reporting experience, due to the pilot's short duration, GRIP did not fully demonstrate that it could reduce the burden on recipients. Similarly, the Federal Demonstration Partnership, whose member universities participated in the GRIP pilot, issued a report. It found that, while using a standard schema increases reporting efficiency, and pre-populating data

---

[21] Federal fund recipients included several institutions of higher education—the University of Washington, the University of Mexico, Colorado State University, the University of Wisconsin, the University of North Carolina System, the College of Lake County, IL—and the city of Bowie, Maryland, and the state of Nebraska. The Environmental Protection Agency and the United States Department of Agriculture also participated in the study.

[22] Recovery Accountability and Transparency Board, Grants Reporting Information Project, Washington, D.C.: June 2013.

can enhance reporting and verify accuracy, at least initially, the pilot did not reduce the burden on recipients.[23]

The GAT Board Is Building on Treasury's Efforts to Integrate Financial Management Systems to Track Spending Better

Information about federal government spending is collected in a complex web of systems and processes that are both overlapping and fragmented. While having standardized data and award identifiers is an important first step to effectively track spending, federal entities also have begun to examine ways to consolidate and streamline data systems that are overlapping or duplicative. The Financial Management Integration and Data Display Working Group is developing recommendations for a work plan that will leverage Treasury's on-going transparency and system modernization efforts.

First, building on Treasury's initiative to standardize payment transaction processes, the Payment Application Modernization project will consolidate more than 30 agency payment systems into a single application. This application will process agency payment requests using Treasury's Standard Payment Request format.[24] All federal agencies that use Treasury disbursing services (Treasury disbursing organizations) will be directed to submit payment data into the newly developed standard format by October 1, 2014. A Treasury official said that federal agencies representing about 142 of 437 agency location codes had either converted to the new format, were testing the new format, or had set a schedule when they would implement the new payment request format. Despite the finding, this official expressed doubt about the ability of some agencies that do not use Treasury for disbursing payments to comply with the data standards by the deadline. The official did note that Treasury continues to provide assistance to these agencies.

---

[23]Federal Demonstration Partnership, Grant Report Information Project: Final Report, Washington, D.C.: May 2013. Available at http://sites.nationalacademies.org/PGA/fdp

[24]Treasury disbursing organizations will be directed to use the Standard Payment Request format to submit detailed payment and accounting data, which in turn will be used to populate the Payment Information Repository. Non-Treasury disbursed agencies will be directed to report detailed payment and accounting data directly to the Payment Information Repository using a different but standard format. Both the Standard Payment Request format used by Treasury disbursed agencies as well as the direct input format used by Non-Treasury disbursed agencies defines the data elements and validation rules that must be used to report payments and associated information into the Payment Information Repository.

Second, the Financial Management Integration and Data Display Working Group is also building on Treasury's initiative to develop a centralized repository containing detailed and summarized records of payment transactions from all federal agencies. The Payment Information Repository will contain data on all payments disbursed by Treasury plus those reported by the Federal agencies that disburse their own payments.[25] This repository will contain descriptive data on those payments for which matching with other data sources (e.g. accounting data, grant data, commercial vendor data, geographic data, etc.) will provide additional information regarding the purpose, program, location and commercial recipient of the payment.

GAT Board Efforts Also Focus on Leveraging Existing Data to Enhance Spending Oversight

A number of government oversight and law enforcement agencies are using data analytics—which involve a variety of techniques to analyze and interpret data to facilitate decision making—to help identify and reduce fraud, waste, and abuse. Data mining applications are emerging as essential tools to inform management decisions, develop government-wide best practices and common solutions, and effectively detect and combat fraud in large programs and investments. For example, predictive analytic technologies can identify fraud and errors before payments are made. Others, such as data-mining and data-matching techniques, can identify fraud or improper payments that have already been awarded. Thus, agencies have help in recovering these dollars. Data mining applications are emerging as essential tools to inform management decisions as well. According to GAT Board officials, making more data available, and doing so in real time, will help agencies make better informed decisions about how they manage federal funds.

The Recovery Board's ROC, established in 2009, uses data analytics to monitor Recovery Act spending to detect and prevent the fraudulent use of funds made available under the act. As part of this effort, ROC analysts use a set of tools that can search large amounts of data from multiple sources. This process is designed to look for patterns and anomalies that could indicate the existence of fraud. The Board has provided several

---

[25]Treasury processes payments for most federal agencies. Thus, it maintains transactional level data on 85 percent of all federal government payments. Non Treasury Disbursing Agencies, including the State Department, HHS, DOD, the Administrative Office of the U.S. Courts, and the Senate, process their own payments but report to Treasury on a non transactional level.

inspectors general with access to these tools through www.FederalAccountability.gov. This site allows inspectors general to review and evaluate entities, such as individuals, companies, and universities, who have received Recovery Act funds. In some cases, ROC staff was able to notify some agencies that they had awarded Recovery funds to companies that were debarred. Thus, these companies should not have received federal funds. For example, ROC analysts found hidden assets that resulted in a court ordering the payment of a fine. They also found several individuals employed by other entities while receiving worker's compensation benefits.

The GAT Board's Data Analytics Working Group has set a goal of expanding on the ROC's work to develop a shared platform for improving fraud detection in federal spending programs. This approach relies on the development of data standards. It will provide a set of analytic tools for fraud detection to be shared across the federal government. Although this work is just starting, working group members have identified several challenges to developing and implementing a shared platform and analytic tools for fraud detection. These challenges include reaching consensus among federal agencies on a set of common data attributes to be used, and changes needed to existing privacy laws to allow access to certain types of protected data and systems.

In January 2013, we convened a forum on data analytics in conjunction with the Council of the Inspectors General on Integrity and Efficiency and the Recovery Board.[26] Its purpose was to explore ways in which oversight and law enforcement agencies use data analytics to detect and prevent fraud, waste, and abuse, and to identify the most significant challenges to realizing the potential of data analytics. Forum participants identified a range of challenges, including technical and legal challenges currently experienced by oversight and law enforcement agencies. In particular, participants highlighted challenges to expanding data sharing within the federal government, including requirements of the Computer Matching and Privacy Protection Act of 1988, as amended,[27] that hindered fraud detection efforts and a lack of data standards and a universal award

---

[26]See GAO, *Highlights of a Forum: Data Analytics for Oversight and Law Enforcement*, GAO-13-680SP. (Washington, D.C.: July 15, 2013).

[27]Agencies' use of certain records when performing certain computer matching programs is subject to statutory safeguards. *See* 5 U.S.C. § 552a(o), (p), (q) and (u).

identifier that limit data sharing across the federal government and across federal, state, and local agencies. Participants also identified opportunities to enhance data-analytics efforts. These opportunities included consolidating data and analytics operations in one location to increase efficiencies by enabling the pooling of resources as well as accessing and sharing of the data.

As Transparency Efforts Get Under Way, Opportunities Remain to Incorporate Lessons Learned from the Recovery Act

The GAT Board's mandated responsibilities include working with the Recovery Board to build on lessons learned and applying approaches developed by the Recovery Board to new efforts to enhance the transparency of federal spending. As discussed above, the GAT Board, the Recovery Board, OMB, and other federal agencies have initiatives under way to improve federal spending transparency. These initiatives include efforts to standardize data and consolidate data systems to improve the accuracy of federal spending and expand oversight of these funds. In many cases these initiatives build on lessons learned from the operation of existing transparency systems, including Recovery.gov and USAspending.gov. However, as new transparency initiatives get under way, opportunities exist to give additional consideration to these lessons to help ensure new transparency programs and policies are implemented successfully.

Lesson One: Standardized Data Enhances Accountability and Supports Systems Integration

One of the key lessons learned from the implementation of the Recovery Act's transparency provisions, was the value of standardized data, including a uniform award identification number for contracts, grants, loans, and other forms of financial assistance. The transparency envisioned under the Recovery Act for tracking spending was unprecedented for the federal government, requiring the development of a system that could track billions of dollars disbursed to thousands of recipients. The system also needed to be operational quickly for a variety of programs, across which even the basic question of what constituted a program or project differed. While agencies had systems that captured such information as award amounts, funds disbursed, and, to varying degrees, progress being made by recipients, the lack of uniform federal data and reporting standards made it difficult to obtain these data from federal agencies. Instead data were collected directly from recipients, which placed additional burden on them to provide these data.

As it developed procedures for reporting on the use of federal funds, OMB directed recipients of covered funds to use a series of standardized data elements. Further, rather than report to multiple government entities, each with its own disparate reporting requirements, all recipients of Recovery funds were required to report centrally into the Recovery Board's inbound reporting website, FederalReporting.gov.[28] According to the GAT Board's 2011 report to the President, the Recovery Board's method for collecting consistent recipient data on spending and posting it rapidly was effective and significantly increased the speed and quality of the spending data reported.[29] The availability of standardized data also allowed the Recovery Board to use data analytics and predictive analysis to detect, prevent, and remediate the fraudulent use of Recovery Act funds. The Recovery Board reported that as a result, the board's analysts were able to find multiple tax liens, regulatory violations, and suspicious financial activity for several companies under investigation by an inspector general. They also were able to notify a number of agencies that they had awarded Recovery funds to companies that were debarred and therefore should not have received federal funds. Initially, the ROC was deployed to detect and prevent fraud under the Recovery Act. In 2012, Congress provided the board the authority to test processes and technologies for monitoring federal spending.[30] As a result, the board—while continuing to maintain its Recovery Act fraud-prevention efforts—has expanded its joint efforts with inspectors general and law enforcement agencies.

As discussed above, the GAT Board had previously identified data standardization, including moving agencies toward a universal, standardized identification system for all federal awards, as a critical step for increased transparency. However, the degree to which data will be standardized across the federal government is still the subject of some debate among Board members. The recent OMB guidance requiring a unique, but not uniform, grant identifier will result in a less standardized approach for grants than contracts. Further, citing agency budgetary constraints and the potential of emerging technologies for extracting non-standard data elements from disparate systems, GAT Board members are taking incremental steps toward increasing data standardization. For example, as the lead agency for the GAT Board's Grants Data

---

[28]OMB, *Updated Guidance on the American Recovery and Reinvestment Act*, M-10-34. (Washington, D.C.: September 24, 2010.

[29]The Government Accountability and Transparency Board, Report and Recommendations to the President (Washington, D.C.: December 2011).

[30]Consolidated Appropriations Act, 2011, Pub. L. No. 112-74, 125 Stat. 786, 920 (2011).

Standardization and Integrity Working Group, OMB asked HHS to analyze the existing level of standardization among grant making agencies, and assess the feasibility and cost of increasing data standards. This analysis examined more than 1,110 individual data elements from more than 17 different sources. It found that there was widespread variation in terminology and associated definitions that impacted how spending was captured, tracked, and reported. In addition, through its work with the GAT Board, Treasury is assessing the potential for implementing new technologies that would allow non-standardized data to be accessed by tagging and linking it to source systems, rather than collecting and warehousing data in a separate system.

Data Standards and Recipient Burden

"Currently, the way the federal reporting system is, it seems very disjointed. At least in our state and in our work in agencies, we're reporting primarily on the same people but in 15 or whatever different reports. So ... standardization would help that, decrease the amount of time that we spend reporting, and a [single] portal would only then make it even more efficient."— *A representative from a nonprofit receiving federal funds*

A lack of uniform standards could also increase the burden on federal fund recipients. Federal fund recipients with whom we spoke told us that the lack of consistent data standards and commonality in how data elements are defined places undue burden on fund recipients because it can result in them having to report the same information multiple times via disparate reporting platforms. Fund recipients also told us that lack of consistent data standards can impact the accuracy of data reported. For example, one higher education official noted that increasing data standardization and reporting consistency across the federal government would eliminate the need for "human intervention" or manual data entry which can impact the accuracy and the timeliness of the data reported. Moreover, collecting data that already exists in agency award systems is also inefficient and burdensome to recipients. Federal fund recipients we spoke to expressed concern about the number of disparate agency and program-specific requirements that obligate them to report the same data multiple times or to report data that should have come from federal sources. These recipients offered a number of suggestions for minimizing reporting redundancy, including limiting data collected from recipients to a small number of essential elements that can only be obtained from recipients, pre-populating electronic reporting forms with data available from agency sources, and using data multiple times rather than requiring that recipients report the same data multiple times.

Lesson Two: Involve Stakeholders in the Development of Reporting Requirements and Guidance

Another key lesson learned from the implementation of Recovery Act reporting requirements was the importance of obtaining and considering the input of stakeholders—federal agencies, recipients, and subrecipients—early in the development of both the reporting system and its procedures. Given the daunting task of rapidly establishing a system to track billions of dollars in Recovery Act funding, OMB and the Recovery Board implemented an iterative process. This process allowed many stakeholders to provide insight into the challenges that could impede their ability to report Recovery Act expenditures. Throughout the development of guidance and in the early months of implementing recipient reporting provisions, OMB and the Recovery Board provided several opportunities for two-way communication with recipients. For example, OMB and the Recovery Board held weekly conference calls with state and local representatives to hear their comments and suggestions, and address their concerns. As a result of these efforts, federal officials changed their plans and related guidance. For example, initial guidance in February 2009 began to lay out information that would be reported on Recovery.gov, and the steps needed to meet reporting requirements, such as including recipient reporting requirements in grant awards and contracts. In response to requests for more clarity, OMB, with input from an array of stakeholders, issued more guidance in June 2009. The guidance clarified requirements on reporting jobs, such as which recipients were required to report, and how to calculate jobs created and retained.

During this current phase of developing transparency efforts, OMB and the GAT Board have implemented a structure to obtain input from a variety of federal stakeholders representing the procurement, grants, and financial management communities. However, mechanisms for obtaining input from non-federal stakeholders are limited to the public rule-making process. The GAT Board's work groups consist of representatives from select federal agencies, OMB, and interagency forums. The work groups are designed to leverage the expertise of federal officials with in-depth knowledge of federal procurement, grant-making, and financial management operations. The Board does not have any formal mechanisms, other than the federal rule-making process, to obtain input from federal fund recipients. An OMB official told us that OMB is leveraging pre-existing personal contacts made during the Recovery Act to obtain feedback from state officials. Further, this official said that OMB had conducted extensive outreach with non-federal stakeholders in seeking their input on OMB's grants reform proposal. These outreach efforts included discussions on standardizing financial information collected during the pre-award and post-award phases of the grant process. However, state officials we spoke with expressed interest in providing additional input into expanding reporting requirements through more formal mechanisms, such as focus or advisory groups. Without a systematic approach for receiving and processing recipients' input, such as the conference calls held for the Recovery Act, issues that could affect recipients' ability to meet new reporting requirements could go unaddressed, compromising the ability of recipients to provide accurate data.

Non-federal stakeholders have been involved in the limited GRIP pilot project discussed above. Recovery Board officials sought feedback from the participating states, a locality, and institutions of higher education throughout the duration of the project through a series of webinars and teleconferences. An online help desk was also established to assist the recipients through the process. At the conclusion of the study, participants were surveyed. They expressed approval for several of the project's aspects, including data standardization, the inclusion of an error-checking feature, and the use of a single central portal for reporting expenditures. Although a Recovery Board official told us that they gained valuable insight from stakeholders through the pilot, they reported that the more inclusive networked community of state and local officials that they established during the Recovery Act implementation had not been sustained.

Federal fund recipients we spoke with underscored the importance of the maintaining the connections they established with federal officials during the implementation of the Recovery Act. They also stressed the importance of having a formal mechanism to provide feedback to the federal government as guidance is crafted and before new transparency reporting requirements are established. Federal fund recipients said that they need clear and understandable guidance to ensure that the data they report are accurate, on time, and minimally burdensome. Officials from organizations representing fund recipients as well as the fund recipients themselves told us that the interactions between OMB and fund recipients during Recovery Act implementation were extremely effective. They noted the frequent communication with OMB staff members who listened to their concerns, addressed questions, and made adjustments to guidance, made it easier for them to report accurate spending data.

Stakeholder Input

"We were really pleased with the level of communication that OMB and the Recovery Board had with us. While we were not always pleased with what they had to say, there would have been more hiccups if we had not had that good communication. Compared with Energy where we were getting inconsistent information, this was consistent guidance. Although all in a crisis mode to get funds out with appropriate accountability, which added lots of pressure, the constant communication provided comfort. It really worked, and should be encouraged, especially in the communication between levels of government."— *An official from an association representing federal fund recipients*

Lesson Three: Delineate Clear Requirements and Lines of Authority for Implementation Efforts

Under the Recovery Act, specific requirements and responsibilities for transparency were clearly laid out in the law, which helped to ensure that transparency requirements were implemented within tight time frames, and thereby provided unprecedented transparency. The Recovery Act specified the timing of reporting, including its frequency and deadlines, and the items that needed to be included in the reporting. The Recovery Board reported that the concrete deadlines imposed by the Recovery Act motivated OMB and the Recovery Board to take action. The Recovery Act required the Recovery Board to conduct and coordinate oversight of the funds provided under the Recovery Act to prevent waste, fraud and abuse, which the Recovery Board accomplished, acting together with OMB, at the federal level to implement the transparency requirements. To implement the recipient reporting requirements, OMB worked with the Recovery Board to deploy a data-collection system at FederalReporting.gov and a public-facing website at Recovery.gov. Further, OMB provided centralized guidance that defined the reporting requirements and the agencies' role in ensuring the quality of data recipients provided. An official from one association representing recipients commented that having information come from one centralized agency, such as OMB, helped assure recipients that their questions were addressed correct. The Recovery Act also provided funding for the Recovery Board, which was used to provide staff and resources for developing and operating its data collection system, website, and data analytic activities.

In contrast, authority for implementing the current transparency initiatives is not as clearly defined. Authority for expanding transparency is centered in an executive order rather than legislation. As we have previously reported, given the importance of leadership to any collaborative effort, transitions and inconsistent leadership, which can occur as administrations change, can weaken the effectiveness of any collaborative efforts, and result in a lack of continuity.[31] According to chairman of the GAT Board, the Board's vision for comprehensive transparency reform will take several years to implement. Therefore, continuity of leadership becomes particularly important. Going forward, changes in the administration and GAT Board membership could hamper the success of future reform efforts if requirements and authorities for

---

[31]GAO, *Managing for Results: Key Considerations for Implementing Interagency Collaborative Mechanisms*, GAO-12-1022 (Washington, D.C.: Sept. 27, 2012).

implementing reforms are not clearly defined in statute. Moreover, the executive order that establishes the GAT Board provides it with a role of setting strategic direction, but not for implementation. As we have previously reported, interagency collaboration on a project, such as expanding transparency, is facilitated when one agency is designated to be accountable, and there are clear roles and responsibilities. This centralizes accountability and can speed decision making in an organization. While there are many officials working together—the GAT Board, work groups led by agency officials, interagency forums such as the Chief Acquisition Officers Council, Council on Financial Assistance Reform and Council of the Inspectors General on Integrity and Efficiency, and OMB—it is not clear where responsibility for implementing the initiatives lies. In oral comments provided on our draft report, OMB staff said that the administration, through its fiscal year 2014 budget proposal, has taken steps to delineate authority by seeking $5.5 million for Treasury to operate and improve the USAspending.gov web site. They believe that this proposal will establish Treasury as single implementing entity for operationalizing transparency reforms.

The lack of clearly delineated authority for implementing initiatives could result in multiple projects working at cross-purposes, overlapping, or missing opportunities to improve transparency consistently. The following represents examples that we gleaned from our interviews and focus groups:

- The GAT Board's Data Analytics work group has been examining approaches to expanding the availability of data to help the oversight community detect and prevent fraud, waste, and abuse in federal programs. Similarly, the Recovery Board's ROC has developed a set of assessment tools that can search large amounts of data from multiple sources to detect fraudulent spending in federal programs. Although the GAT Board's mandate includes a requirement for it to work with the Recovery Board to apply the approaches developed by the latter across the federal government, the extent to which the work of the ROC is being incorporated into the GAT Board's effort to develop approaches for using data analytics to improve oversight is unclear.
- The GAT Board and the Recovery Board have similar projects under way to standardize grants data elements and procedures. The GAT Board's Grants Data Standardization and Integrity Working Group is identifying approaches to standardize key data elements to improve the accuracy of grants award data. The Recovery Board's GRIP pilot examined whether a uniform award identification number could be

used to track grants expenditures throughout the grant life cycle. However, it is unclear whether the study's results will be incorporated into the work of the Grants Data Standardization and Integrity Working Group, which could lead to inefficiencies caused by duplicated efforts.

Moreover, without operational authority, the GAT Board must leverage the authorities and networks of its individual members. Thus, the successful implementation of transparency initiatives depends on the willingness and capacity of individual members' agencies to drive this change, and may not be sustainable. For example, the GAT Board chairman used his position on the FAR Council to have it consider and vote on a proposed rule that will require all federal agencies to use a uniform procurement identification number for all of its solicitations and awards. The GAT Board chairman drove this initiative based on his capacity as Director of the Defense Procurement and Acquisition Policy Office at DOD. However, the extent to which this governance structure will be effective or sustainable over time is limited to and dependent upon those existing connections.

Unlike under the Recovery Act, these transparency initiatives are being funded through existing agency resources using agency personnel, as separate funding is unavailable. While the GAT Board lacks funding of its own, it relies on agencies to develop approaches to improve data transparency. Agency officials we spoke with said they expect that automation and standardization mechanisms embedded in transparency initiatives now under way could help federal agencies to more efficiently and effectively manage their activities and programs. Efficiencies and economies generated by these initiatives might have the potential to save money, and thereby lessen the need for appropriations or other forms of dedicated funding. In the short term, the GAT Board believes it can continue to make incremental changes by leveraging ongoing agency initiatives.

Conclusions

Ensuring the transparency of more than $3.7 trillion in federal spending annually, including more than $1 trillion awarded through contracts, grants, and loans, and an additional $1 trillion in forgone revenue from tax expenditures is an important national goal. Efforts to improve transparency of spending data continue to involve multiple federal entities, under the strategic leadership of the GAT Board and OMB. Meanwhile, the Recovery Board continues to play a role in evaluating new approaches to collecting data and maintaining systems to use the data for ensuring accountability. However, roles and responsibilities for the effort are not clearly delineated. For example, under the Recovery Act, authority to mandate requirements was centered in OMB and the Recovery Board, and was clearly delineated and funded, whereas under the current transparency initiatives, the leadership for implementing actions is spread across several agencies, knitted together loosely under the GAT Board's strategic direction. Given the importance of clear requirements and consistent leadership for ensuring recommended approaches are institutionalized across the federal government and progress is sustained over the long-term, the present governance structure for transparency efforts could hamper planned advancements. Having clear requirements and implementation authority, particularly through legislation, will help ensure effective and sustained implementation of transparency efforts across the federal government.

While the transparency initiatives under way represent a promising start, insights could be gleaned from lessons learned from the operation of Recovery.gov. Such insights would ensure that new approaches are implemented consistently across the federal government, and progress toward strategic goals can be sustained long term. As OMB and the GAT Board take incremental steps to improve data transparency and expand oversight of federal spending, it will be important to develop a long-term vision and concrete plan for improving transparency, and ensure its implementation. For example, a key lesson learned from the implementation of the Recovery Act was the importance of data standards, including a universal award identifier to enable the tracking of Recovery Act spending, and a uniform numbering system for identifying federal awards would improve the tracking of all federal spending. Moreover, by listening to stakeholders during Recovery Act implementation, OMB and the Recovery Board heard concerns and made changes to plans and guidance accordingly. As new transparency initiatives are developed, the input of all stakeholders, including nonfederal entities such as state and local governments, would help OMB and the GAT Board to identify approaches that minimize the burden on those doing the reporting, and address reporting challenges. Although the non-federal stakeholders are a broad and diverse group, as future changes are considered, it will be important to identify mechanisms to involve stakeholders as early as possible.

Recommendations for Executive Action

We recommend that the Director of OMB, in collaboration with the members of the GAT Board, take the following two actions:

- Develop a plan to implement comprehensive transparency reform, including a long-term timeline and requirements for data standards, such as establishing a uniform award identification system across the federal government.
- Increase efforts for obtaining input from stakeholders, including entities receiving federal funds, to address reporting challenges, and strike an appropriate balance that ensures the accuracy of the data without unduly increasing the burden on those doing the reporting.

Matter for Congressional Consideration

To ensure effective decision making and the efficient use of resources dedicated to enhancing the transparency of federal spending data, Congress should consider legislating transparency requirements and establish clear lines of authority to ensure that recommended approaches for improving spending data transparency are implemented across the federal government.

Agency Comments and Our Evaluation

We provided a draft of this report to the Director of OMB, the GAT Board and the Recovery Board Chairs, the Administrator of GSA, and the Secretaries of HHS, DOD, and Treasury for review and comment. OMB provided oral comments, which are summarized below. HHS provided general comments that are also discussed below. In addition, the GAT Board and DOD concurred with our recommendations and provided technical comments, as well as additional clarifying information related to the recommendations. Treasury generally agreed with our findings and provided technical comments, while the Recovery Board and GSA provided technical comments only.

In its oral comments, OMB staff indicated that they generally concurred with our findings and recommendations. Regarding our recommendation for developing a long-term plan for implementing data standards, OMB staff agreed that the GAT Board's plan provides an initial strategy and added that multiple initiatives are under way. One of these initiatives is the administration's fiscal year 2014 budget proposal that would operationalize comprehensive transparency through the transfer of USAspending.gov from GSA to Treasury. We have provided additional information on this in the report. For our recommendation on increasing efforts to obtain stakeholder input as transparency initiatives are developed, OMB staff agreed that increasing efforts to obtain stakeholder input was important and pointed to their outreach to date particularly in seeking stakeholder comments on the grants reform process, which they said included discussions on standardizing financial information collected from recipients during the pre-award and post-award phases of the grant process. We have provided additional information in this report on this as well. We continue to believe, however, that as specific proposals for transparency initiatives are being developed, additional mechanisms need to be in place to provide two-way communication to ensure that reporting challenges are addressed without unduly increasing reporting burden. OMB generally agreed with our matter for congressional consideration on legislating transparency requirements, but noted that the Congress has provided a robust statutory framework through legislation, such as FFATA and the GPRA Modernization Act of 2010, and therefore additional legislation is unnecessary. However, as we have previously concluded, given the importance of clear requirements and consistent leadership for ensuring approaches are institutionalized and sustained over the long term, legislation will help ensure effective implementation of comprehensive transparency reform.

The comments submitted by the HHS Assistant Secretary for Legislation stressed the need to recognize the impact of data standardization on agency operations and resources, and noted that the overarching federal vision for transparency must articulate both the long term goals, as well as more operational and pragmatic steps to be taken in order to achieve such goals. HHS also underscored the importance of coming to an agreement on the range of federal spending information that is needed to achieve transparency and on which data elements are mandatory for reporting and for information collection requirements.

We are sending copies of this report to the appropriate congressional committees and the Recovery Board and GAT Board Chairs, the Director of OMB, the Secretaries of HHS, DOD, and Treasury, and the Administrator of GSA.

If you or your staff has any questions concerning this report, please contact me at (202) 512-6806 or czerwinskis@gao.gov. Contact points for our Offices of Congressional Relations and Public Affairs may be found on the last page of this report. Key contributors are listed in appendix IV.

Stanley J. Czerwinski
Director, Strategic Issues

List of Requesters

The Honorable Thomas R. Carper
Chairman
Committee on Homeland Security and Governmental Affairs
United States Senate

The Honorable Tom Coburn, MD
Ranking Member
Committee on Homeland Security and Governmental Affairs
United States Senate

The Honorable Mark R. Warner
Member
Committee on the Budget
United States Senate

The Honorable Claire McCaskill
Chairman
Subcommittee on Financial and Contracting Oversight
United States Senate

The Honorable Susan M. Collins
United States Senate

Appendix I: Objectives, Scope, and Methodology

We were asked to examine efforts to increase the transparency of federal spending data, and identify lessons from the experience of operating existing data systems that could help increase federal spending data transparency. To accomplish this, we (1) reviewed federal initiatives to improve the accuracy and availability of federal spending data; and (2) assessed the extent to which lessons identified by GAO and federal fund recipients from the operation of Recovery.gov and USAspending.gov are being addressed by these new transparency initiatives.

To address these objectives, we examined data collection and reporting requirements under FFATA and the Recovery Act, the June 2011 Executive Order that established the GAT Board, Executive Order 13,576, "Delivering an Efficient, Effective, and Accountable Government," relevant OMB guidance and memoranda, such as OMB-10-06, Open Government Directive and Improving Data Quality for USAspending.gov, and reports outlining action plans and recommendations created by the GAT Board, the Recovery Board, and other federal entities charged with developing approaches to improve federal data transparency.

We interviewed officials at OMB, the GAT Board, and the Recovery Board who are examining new data transparency approaches. We also interviewed officials at three agencies who represent the perspectives of the federal procurement, grant, and financial management communities, and who are working with the GAT Board to build on transparency initiatives under way within their agencies that could be applied across the federal government: DOD, HHS, and Treasury, respectively. We also interviewed officials at GSA, the agency that manages USAspending.gov, to gain their perspectives on the challenges associated with ensuring the quality of the data submitted to this site.

To capture the perspective of the federal fund recipients, we conducted a series of interviews with officials from organizations representing federal fund recipients and government reform organizations. We wanted to get their perspectives on lessons learned from the operation of existing transparency systems, and federal efforts under way to improve data transparency. We selected these associations because our preliminary research indicated that they had either been involved in Recovery Act implementation, had published reports related to the Recovery Act, had expressed official positions on existing transparency systems, or had submitted official statements on pending legislation designed to improve transparency. To capture a wide range of recipient perspectives, we also selected associations that represented a variety of recipient types, from state and local governments, nonprofit organizations, and contractors. For

this review, we interviewed and collected comments from officials at the
following organizations:

- National Association of State Auditors, Comptrollers, and Treasurers
- National Association of State Budget Officers
- National Association of Counties
- Federal Demonstration Partnership
- National Council of Nonprofits
- National Association of State Chief Information Officers
- Council on Government Relations
- Professional Services Council
- Center for Effective Government
- Project on Government Oversight
- Sunlight Foundation

We also conducted seven focus groups representing a range of federal
fund recipients.[1] Focus groups included: (1) state comptrollers and
budget officials; (2) state education and transportation officials; (3) local
government officials from both large and small municipalities; and (4)
nonprofit organizations, research universities, and representatives from
business who contract with the federal government. Each focus group
had between four and eight participants who were recruited from
randomized member lists provided by the recipient associations we
interviewed. We audio-recorded the focus groups, transcribed the
recordings, and analyzed the findings with qualitative analysis software
for common themes and pattern.

Finally, we reviewed our previous work on the reporting successes and
challenges experienced by both agencies and federal fund recipients.
This process was designed to identify lessons learned from those
experiences that should be considered as new approaches to data
transparency are developed.

We conducted this performance audit from November 2012 to September
2013 in accordance with generally accepted government auditing
standards. Those standards require that we plan and perform the audit to
obtain sufficient, appropriate evidence to provide a reasonable basis for
our findings and conclusions based on our audit objectives. We believe

---

[1]Results from nongeneralizable samples cannot be used to make inferences about a
population.

that the evidence obtained provides a reasonable basis for our findings and conclusions based on our audit objectives.

Appendix II: Government Accountability and Transparency Board and Work Group Agency Partners

The Government Accountability and Transparency Board (GAT Board) is composed of the following 11 members designated by the President from among agency Inspectors General, agency Chief Financial Officers or Deputy Secretaries, and senior officials from OMB. The President designates a Chairman from among the members.

- Director, Defense Procurement and Acquisition Policy, U.S. Department of Defense
- Inspector General, U.S. Postal Service
- Assistant Secretary, Department of the Treasury
- Inspector General, U.S. Department of Energy
- Deputy Secretary, U.S. Department of Veterans Affairs
- Inspector General, National Science Foundation
- Inspector General, U.S. Department of Health and Human Services
- Assistant Secretary for Financial Resources and Chief Financial Officer, U.S. Department of Health and Human Services
- Inspector General, U.S. Department of Transportation
- Inspector General, U.S. Department of Education
- Deputy Controller, Office of Management and Budget

The GAT Board established four working groups, as shown in table 1.

Table 1: Composition and Purpose of the GAT Board Working Groups

Working group	Working group members	Purpose
Procurement Data Standardization and Integrity	• Department of Defense (Lead) • Office of Federal Procurement Policy (OMB) • Chief Acquisition Officers Council	Identify approaches for standardizing contract data elements and electronic transactions to ensure data accuracy and enable the tracking of contract transactions from purchase order through vendor payment.
Grants Data Standardization and Integrity	• Department of Health and Human Services (Lead) • Office of Federal Financial Management (OMB) • Council on Financial Assistance Reform	Identify approaches to standardize grants data elements to achieve great consistency across the federal government
Financial Management Integration and Data Display	• Department of Treasury • Office of Federal Financial Management (OMB)	Identify approaches for linking the financial management data maintained in agency financial systems with agency awards data in order to improve the quality of the data displayed to the public.
Data Analytics	• United States Postal Service (Lead) • Recovery Board	Expand upon the work of the Recovery Board's Recovery Operation Center to develop a shared platform to improve fraud detection in federal spending programs

Source: GAO analysis of GAT Board Documents

Appendix III: Comments from the Department of Health and Human Services

DEPARTMENT OF HEALTH & HUMAN SERVICES

OFFICE OF THE SECRETARY

Assistant Secretary for Legislation
Washington, DC 20201

AUG 3 0 2013

Stanley J. Czerwinski
Director, Strategic Issues
U.S. Government Accountability Office
441 G Street NW
Washington, DC 20548

Dear Mr. Czerwinski,

Attached are comments on the U.S. Government Accountability Office's (GAO) report entitled, "Federal Data Transparency: Opportunities Remain to Incorporate Lessons Learned as Availability of Spending Data Increases" (GAO-13-758).

The Department appreciates the opportunity to review this report prior to publication.

Sincerely,

Jim R. Esquea
Assistant Secretary for Legislation

Attachment

**GENERAL COMMENTS OF THE DEPARTMENT OF HEALTH AND HUMAN
SERVICES (HHS) ON THE GOVERNMENT ACCOUNTABILITY OFFICE'S (GAO)
DRAFT REPORT ENTITLED, "FEDERAL DATA TRANSPARENCY:
OPPORTUNITIES REMAIN TO INCORPORATE LESSONS LEARNED AS
AVAILABILITY OF SPENDING DATA INCREASES (GAO-13-758)**

The Department appreciates the opportunity to review and comment on this draft report.

The Department of Health and Human Services (HHS) is committed to promoting greater
financial transparency across the federal community through data standardization and
coordinated outreach to stakeholders. As noted in the report, HHS and other federal agencies
continue this path forward; however, we note that certain matters will require additional
consideration, analysis and resolution.

- Scope of needed information: In order to manage the data standardization efforts,
  achieve system and implementation-related efficiencies, and reduce administrative
  reporting burdens, it is important to come to an agreement on the range of federal
  spending information that is needed to achieve transparency and on which data elements
  are mandatory for reporting and for information collection requirements, versus those that
  are agency specific and/or optional.

- Impact to agency operations and resources: As existing data elements and associated
  definitions are standardized, and new data elements integrated, agencies will need to
  understand and address the impacts to their respective operations, processes, and
  reporting systems. Resources will likely be required to update business processes and
  systems; and training will likely be required to ensure data elements are understood and
  properly reported. To this end, the overarching federal vision for transparency must
  articulate both the long term goals, as well as more operational and pragmatic steps to be
  taken in order to achieve such goals.

- Timely collection and processing of information: Data quality and transparency not only
  hinge upon complete and accurate information, but also timely receipt of that
  information. The input, reconciliation and reporting of data must occur within a
  compressed timeframe to enable the agency to make informed decisions based on this
  information and provide the desired transparency. While accuracy, completeness and
  timeliness of information are the foundations of data quality metrics, agencies will need
  to balance receipt of timely information with recipient burden and streamline internal
  business processes to facilitate the timely processing of information.

- Data analytics: Data analytics have been used in past projects with positive results. HHS
  agrees that data analytics should be part of the longer-term transparency vision.

- Leveraging existing processes: Similar to the efforts to standardize and improve
  transparency across contracts data is being advanced through the Federal Acquisition
  Regulatory Council, the longer-term transparency vision must take into account existing
  data standardization processes, and leverage their progress, best practices, and knowledge
  as appropriate.

1

GENERAL COMMENTS OF THE DEPARTMENT OF HEALTH AND HUMAN
SERVICES (HHS) ON THE GOVERNMENT ACCOUNTABILITY OFFICE'S (GAO)
DRAFT REPORT ENTITLED, "FEDERAL DATA TRANSPARENCY:
OPPORTUNITIES REMAIN TO INCORPORATE LESSONS LEARNED AS
AVAILABILITY OF SPENDING DATA INCREASES (GAO-13-758)

The Department appreciates being recognized by the Government Accountability Office for its
leadership role in the grants data standardization effort. Moreover, we recognize the critical
nature of our responsibilities as members of the Government Accountability and Transparency
(GAT) Board, Chief Acquisition Officers' Council, and Council on Financial Assistance
Reform; and the role of these organizations in achieving the long term transparency vision.

2

Appendix IV: GAO Contact and Staff Acknowledgments

GAO Contact	Stanley J. Czerwinski, (202) 512-6806 or czerwinskis@gao.gov
Staff Acknowledgments	In addition to the contact named above, Carol L. Patey, Assistant Director, and Kathleen M. Drennan, Ph.D., Analyst-in-Charge, supervised the development of this report. Gerard S. Burke and Patricia Norris made significant contributions to all aspects of this report. Cynthia M. Saunders, Ph.D. assisted with the design and methodology, Andrew J. Stephens provided legal counsel, Robert Robinson developed the report's graphics, and Jessica Nierenberg, Judith Kordahl, and Keith O'Brien verified the information in this report. Other important contributors included James R. Sweetman, Jr., Michael S. LaForge, William T. Woods, and Tatiana Winger.

www.ingramcontent.com/pod-product-compliance
Lightning Source LLC
Chambersburg PA
CBHW080629290526
45790CB00007B/2988